Good Morning Girls

LEADER'S MANUAL

By Courtney Joseph

TABLE OF CONTENTS

Welcome GMG Leaders!

Thank you for taking the initiative to lead a group! There is so much you will do to encourage and serve your group that no one but God will ever see. Thank you in advance!

There will be times when your group may be quiet. Do not be discouraged. This is normal. Even my own group has gone through valleys and hard transitions.

THESE ARE OUR VALUES AT GMG:

- We value deep conversation seasoned with grace.

- We value trust and privacy.

- We value respect of one another and different convictions.

- We value unity and encourage private discussion outside of the group to resolve matters.

- We value gentle input and encouragement.

- We value patience and grace with one another.

- We value honesty. If you need to depart the group please let the group know rather than be silent.

- We value you and your walk with the King!

Please share these values with the group to set the tone at the start.

I can't wait to see how God works in our lives!

Thank you for joining us on this journey!

Keep Walking With the King,

Courtney

The GMG Statement of Belief

Women Living Well Ministries is a non-denominational, evangelical ministry.

THIS IS OUR STATEMENT OF FAITH:

We believe that the Bible is God's inspired, infallible, and inerrant Word and is the sole written revelation that rules the faith and practice for all Christians and alone can bind the conscience. We believe that God has preserved His Word and that by His power it has been kept from being lost, destroyed, or diluted with error (2 Timothy 3:16; Psalm 119:89; 1 Peter 1:23, 25).

We believe in one God, Creator of all things, perfect in love and holiness, who exists as three Persons: Father, Son, and Holy Spirit (Matthew 28:19; 2 Corinthians 13:14; Peter 1:2).

We believe that Jesus Christ is fully God and entered human form by the miracle of the Virgin Birth, that He lived a sinless life, and that He died for our sins. Christ is the only mediator through whose work we are redeemed. We believe that He rose again on the third day and now sits at the right hand of God as our Advocate (Matthew 1:18-25; John 1:1, 14, 3:16; 1 Corinthians 15:3-7; 1 Timothy 2:5; Hebrews 1:3; 1 John 2:1).

We believe that the Holy Spirit is God. His ministry is to glorify the Lord Jesus Christ and convict the world of sin, righteousness, and judgment. We believe that He brings about the new birth, indwells, baptizes, seals, anoints, and endows all who are regenerated with spiritual gifts. The Holy Spirit also leads believers who daily surrender their life to Him by guiding, teaching, sanctifying, and filling them (John 15:26, 16:8, 3:3-6, 14:16-17, 14:26).

We believe that all people are created in the image of God. At the same time, because of Adam's sin, all people are sinful by nature and choice. Apart from forgiveness through Jesus Christ, all are lost and alienated from God (Genesis 1:27, 3:1-6; Romans 3:23; Ephesians 2:1-3).

We believe that salvation rests solely on the work of God's grace for us and in us. We are justified by grace through faith alone. Christ's death is the only payment for sin that God will accept. Additionally, the righteousness of Christ is transferred to us by faith and is the only merit or righteousness that God will accept—we possess the righteousness of Christ in the sight of God (Romans 3:23-26, 4:1-3). All who truly believe in Christ are born again and become the children of God (John 1:12-13; Ephesians 2:8-9). All true believers, once saved, are kept by God's power, not our own, and are thus secure in Christ forever (John 6:37-40, 10:27-30; Romans 8:1, 38-39).

We believe in the resurrection of the body. At death the spirits of the saved go immediately to be with the Lord Jesus Christ in Heaven, and the unsaved descend immediately into Hell until the final Day of Judgment. At that time, their bodies shall be raised from the grave: the saved will return to be in Heaven with Christ, the lost will be judged and returned to Hell (Luke 16:19-31, 23:43; Revelation 20:11-15).

We believe that the Church consists of all who believe in Jesus Christ as Savior. The local church exists to exalt Christ, encourage believers, and evangelize the world. We believe that every local church is free to govern its own affairs under Christ and should seek to support the unity of all Christ-honoring churches and ministries (Colossians 1:28; Ephesians 4:3-6).

WHY I NEED TO KNOW THE GOOD MORNING GIRLS STATEMENT OF BELIEF

It is a privilege for Good Morning Girls to welcome women from all walks of life, with varying backgrounds and experiences. The women who make up Good Morning Girls come from all over the world, painting a picture of God's love of diversity. Yet something each Good Morning Girl has in common is a sisterhood in Jesus Christ and a passion to know God more through His Word.

Some have walked with God for much of their lives, and others are learning- some for the very first time—the beautiful truths of what it means to be a follower of Jesus Christ. We can learn so much from each other!

With that excitement comes much responsibility as well. Our desire at Good Moring Girls is that every woman would base their knowledge of God on truth. While denominations and preferences of each GMG may differ, our passion is to come together in unity under the sole authority of God's Word. For this reason, we have a GMG Statement of Belief.

So, why do you as a leader, need to know the Good Morning Girls Statement of Belief? So you can be aware, when your identify yourself with GMG, what truth you are standing for, and can confidently be equipped to lead women in your group on the basis of that truth.

If you ever have questions about where Good Morning Girls stands on a doctrine, please use this Statement of Belief as your guide.

If there is a doctrine not mentioned, please remember to stick to the topics that unite us, and not divide us.

Leader's Responsibilities

"Good Morning Girls" is a group of Christian women who keep each other accountable in their quiet times through email, Facebook, text messaging, Instagram, blogging, group meetings or any other means.

As a GMG leader, we ask that you form a group of women, who are interested in being accountable, as they study the Bible together. God knew that we would need the encouragement of other believers.

A leader is not only responsible for forming a group, but for keeping it going.

Leaders are faithful encouragers who can commit to at least the time frame of the current GMG session (Fall, Winter, Spring or Summer). While all group members keep each other accountable in Bible reading, your group members will look to you as the leader for consistency in communicating, and as a resource for study information.

WE ENCOURAGE LEADERS TO:

- Do your Bible Study. Set the example for your group by getting in the Word daily. It is hard to ask others to do something you are not doing yourself.

- Pray for your leadership and for group members regularly. The prayer of the righteous is powerful and effective. (James 5:16)

- Communicate regularly with your GMG group. They want to hear from you. They often need you to be the one to initiate contact.

- Create trust within your group. Maintain a level of confidentiality.

- Be an encourager. Accountability is much more effective when someone is cheering you on.

- Practice humility and honesty. Transparency in leadership often encourages members to open up and share their own victories and struggles in their walk with God.

- Use the resources available to you out on the blog at **www.WomenLivingWell.org**. You can find all the resources for past and current studies under the Good Morning Girls Resources tab.

- Most importantly, depend on God. Seek Him first. Listen to His direction for your group.

How do I set up a Good Morning Girls Group?

All Good Morning Girls groups are different, meeting the needs of different women, at different seasons of life.

As the leader, you get to pick the outlet that will work best for you. Facebook, Instagram, Twitter, Email, Facebook Groups or group meetings in your home or at your church, are all options. Be creative! Because GMG involves accountability, it is necessary that all group members have access to the mode of communication you choose.

We regroup a few times a year. Usually it is in the winter, spring, summer and fall. This allows a graceful bow out time for women who need to leave your group who might have studies going on in their local church or who are not able to commit.

Good Morning Girls does not seek to come in place of the local church but it does provide a resource for women at local churches to use. It also is for women who might not have a Bible Study available for them in their local body or who can't attend because of their stage of life.

Good Morning Girls groups come in all shapes and sizes. Some groups might be small, with personal girlfriends from your church or playgroup, family members, high school or college friends or even co-workers. These groups might even meet in person. We love and encourage that! Other groups might be larger in nature, and often exist on Facebook to accommodate anyone who is looking for accountability. This also allows flexibility in schedules. People can share when they are free and not feel tied down to a set time and place. Group members can live anywhere on the planet, and with the beauty of the internet, they can connect and be accountable.

While it takes no set number of women to form a group, Good Moring Girls suggests that a group of 4-12 is ideal.

This includes enough members to keep the group going, yet it is still small enough to encourage intimacy and sharing. We have found that bigger groups are not always better since they tend to lose their intimate feel and the women begin to feel like a number in a crowd or they won't share their personal details.

I Have Members ~ What's Next?

Hooray! You have members. Now, what's next?

1. CREATE A WELCOME LETTER.

Have a welcome letter in your group so that all your ladies can get to know you and know what to expect. We have a welcome letter available on page 16 of this manual. Feel free to tweak this letter and make it your own or come up with something great yourself.

2. SHARE EXPECTATIONS.

Make sure your ladies know the expectations of the group. Good Morning Girls provides a daily reading plan and a discussion question each day. You could post your SOAK reflections in the morning and the discussion question at night or maybe you won't use the discussion questions (which is up to you). Just let your ladies know what they can expect. We suggest you post study information at the same time. Some ladies like to upload the whole study for the week (if using Facebook) on Sunday, and then it is easier to keep up with during the week. Some like to post each day. Just make sure you know the time zone of the ladies in your group so the information is up when it is morning for them!

3. SUBSCRIBE TO THE BLOG AND LIKE THE GMG FACEBOOK PAGE.

You will want to encourage your ladies to subscribe to the Women Living Well Blog and LIKE the Good Morning Girls Facebook page. These pages will offer great encouragement for them.

4. ENCOURAGE YOUR GROUP TO DOWNLOAD THE RESOURCES.

On the Good Morning Girls Resources tab, on the Women Living Well blog, are some great resources that are free. There are reading plans, bookmarks, color coding pages, and more!

5. SHARE THE JOURNALS.

Good Morning Girls has journals you can buy on Amazon. These are not devotionals; however, they do have a verse of the day, a synopsis of the book we are studying, and the discussion questions in written form.

6. CREATE OPPORTUNITIES FOR THE GROUP MEMBERS TO MEET EACH OTHER.

Help your ladies get to know each other. Post icebreaker questions (found in this manual) and ask them to introduce themselves. Perhaps they will share a picture of their family. Just stick to topics that can unite us and not divide us. Topics of division include television and movie choices and politics.

Tips to Help Your GMG Group Thrive

Good Morning Girls groups help encourage women to be in the Word of God daily. Another benefit is the encouragement that women can receive from other women in the body of Christ, as we walk through life together.

God made us to desire relationships, first with Him, and then with others. With a Good Morning Girls group, we can help develop both of those kinds of relationships.

Here are a few things you can do to help your GMG group thrive:

1. GET TO KNOW EACH OTHER.

Go deeper. Initiate conversations about hobbies, goals, families, passions and personal testimonies. These things will help the ladies connect with other women in the group, and will encourage each other. Creating intimacy starts with you as the leader.

2. PRAY FOR EACH OTHER.

When you pray for others, your heart connects at a deeper level. Be sure to share prayer request daily and follow up with other group member's requests.

3. ENCOURAGE COMMITMENT.

Accountability is key, and you should lead by example.

4. CREATE A POSITIVE, WELCOMING ATMOSPHERE.

There is enough negativity in our world. Do your part to make your group a safe and encouraging place to be. Be especially attentive to those who may not feel like they "fit in". They need it the most.

5. SHARE STUDY GOALS WITH EACH OTHER, AND ENCOURAGE EACH OTHER IN YOUR SPIRITUAL WALK.

Remember why you created this group and why the women joined.

6. KEEP CHRIST THE CENTER OF ALL YOU DO.

Make goals and keep each other accountable. Stick to topics that unite and don't divide.

7. HAVE FUN! LAUGHTER IS THE BEST MEDICINE.

Make sure you provide moments in your group that are fun. Share funny stories, recipes, or birthdays. If you live close to each other, make plans to get together for coffee, dinner, or playgroups. The activity doesn't matter as much as the fellowship.

8. STICK TO THE TRUTH OF THE WORD OF GOD.

Be on guard against personal agendas. Instead, let God be the focus.

How to Encourage Participation

The whole idea of GMG is to keep each other accountable in our quiet times. In order to do that, we need group members who participate. We have found that you can encourage participation in several ways, and we hope you will come up with ideas of your own, as you get to know your group.

- Take the lead and be the first to communicate with your group every day. They will hopefully follow your lead and many will not post if they don't think you are going to.

- Initiate discussions on how to apply the daily verses to your life, in a practical way.

- Engage with what others are saying. Comment on what they share. Tag them, or specifically mention their post. They want to know you are interacting with their comments. It makes them feel valuable to the group.

- Ask questions.

- Include the daily verses in your message, so that even if a lady doesn't get into the reading, she at least is being exposed to the scripture by reading what you wrote.

- Contact your group members and encourage them personally. Remember some may respond better to a private message, email or phone call and will appreciate that you took the time to reach out.

Members who are well cared for tend to participate more often.

Keeping a Healthy Perspective

Even the most organized, well thought-out groups will experience times when participation wanes. Don't get discouraged leaders!

When communication seems silent, keep posting and encouraging your members. You may be surprised to find out that the silent member is going through a difficult time or feels like she has nothing more to add to the discussion, or is slightly intimidated by other's comments.

Some ladies might be new to the Bible, or not even be believers. On top of that, women can get very busy with the many responsibilities that they carry.

Our desire at GMG is not to judge, but to encourage. Only God knows the heart. We have heard story after story of women growing in their relationships with God through GMG, even when they are not vocal in their groups. Women have accepted Christ as their Savior, even after being silent in their GMG group. Just because they don't communicate does not mean they are not reading and gleaning from others.

Don't give up! The benefits you can receive from simply being in the Word yourself, is worth it to keep going. God will reward your effort as you seek to know Him more.

We pray for you often. You are a vital member of this ministry—we could not do it without you. Our desire is that GMG would be a beautiful example of what God can do through the Body of Christ.

Fostering an Atmosphere of Community

One thing that women are looking for, when they join a group with Good Morning Girls, is community. It is up to us as leaders to create this environment in our groups. We want all the women, who come to our groups, to feel like they are included.

It's important to start with introductions at the start of each new study. If you have formed a Facebook Group, you can post a picture for them to comment on, or a document that everyone adds information to. If you are doing an email group, have each lady send an email and introduce herself. Have them include pictures of their family.

You set the tone for these introductions by being the first one to introduce yourself. Keep it short and sweet. As other ladies are introducing themselves, look for common threads where you can relate to the women in your group. Then, begin icebreaker questions (there are a list of these at the back of this manual).

Be sure to interact with women as they participate. You can keep it simple by tagging them and saying things like "Great thought!" "Thanks for sharing that!" "Love your insight". These phrases are ways that you can encourage your ladies. They will know that you read what they said and that it has value to the group's discussion.

Take note of prayer request and remember to go back and ask how they are doing. You can do this through a private message or email, or even through the group wall on Facebook. Let them know that you are praying and ask for updates. If you are comfortable, write out your prayer so they can read it. Reading a written prayer is very powerful and lets them know you did what you said you would do.

Do some fun things with your groups. This works best in smaller groups. Use icebreakers on Fridays to keep fun conversation going throughout the weekend. Use the holidays as conversation starters. Stay away from politics, television, or other topics that could divide your group.

You should use caution in flooding the group with things that are not related to the study. Make sure you keep the main point Bible study. Use the other things like icing—just a little goes a long way!

Every group is a unique blend of women and personalities, but we have found God brings the women together that need one another. Some groups connect quickly, and others take time. Some groups stay together for years and others for just one session. Our job is to foster an environment where friendships can be formed and women feel open to share. Our job is to share, encourage and pray.

Share what God is teaching you, from your heart. Your openness will encourage other to share what they are learning. Pray for the ladies God has given you. Encourage the women to share—and be ready to watch God do amazing things!

The Importance of Prayer

Jesus Christ is the foundation of your group. Prayer is the first block that you can build on. Before women ever share what God is teaching them, they will share prayer requests. Groups that actively participate in prayer for their members are far more active and develop a greater bond.

Prayer is necessary and helps us grow in our individual faith and to reach out to others. Even unbelievers will often want us to pray for them, but not want to engage in talk about the Bible. We can open doors by praying for people.

As leaders, it is important that we cover our groups in prayer. Begin praying for your group before it forms. As the ladies start to join your group, add them to your prayer list.

Remember that prayer requests are confidential. Once all your members are in your group, and you start sharing prayer requests, your group (if on Facebook) should be set to secret. Remind the ladies in your group that prayer requests are confidential. Also, be on guard for gossip in the form of a prayer request.

Prayer should be a community builder. When you say you are going to pray for someone, be sure to do it. Check back in with them. Feel free to type your prayer out for them—this gives the person with the request comfort knowing that they were in fact prayed for. Prayer can be a bonding factor and help bring us closer together as we walk through real life situations with the people in our groups.

As you begin to pray for the request in your group, you will see your ladies follow through in praying for others also.

Besides prayer requests, be sure that you pray daily for God to grow the women in your group as they walk with him. If they have not shared a prayer request, pray that they would grow spiritually, that they would not fall into temptation and that they would be safe. Use the beginning of the Epistles of Paul to find things he prayed for the churches and use those verses to pray over the ladies God has given you.

Sample Welcome Letter

Hello Ladies!

My name is _____, and I am so excited to be your GMG leader!

I have prayed for you. I am excited to dive deep into God's Word with you this session!

A little bit about me...I am ____ years old, and have been married to my wonderful husband _____ for ____ years. We have _____ children. Their names are _____, _____, and _____.

We live in _____ and attend _____ church.

I have a passion for the Word of God, children, writing/blogging, crafting, photography, traveling, coffee, sunsets, cooking, and _____ ____.

I'm so excited to start this next Good Morning Girls session with all of you. This smaller, intimate group is an excellent way to stay better connected. I pray that God will give us wisdom and insight each day as we look into His Word. Please be ready to share what God is teaching you. I know we all benefit from what each person shares. In fact, the purpose of this group is to share. Write comments, read comments and like comments. Try to check in daily if you can.

DAILY BIBLE STUDY AND CHECK-IN:

Here's how it will work. Each day, I will post the reading of the day and you will post what you got from your daily quiet time. There is also a daily discussion question. If you are having a hard time finding something specific to share, this question should help you have a jumping point.

SOAK

There is a greater explanation in the study guide. But if you are not inclined to use the SOAK method, just do it your own way. We just want to know what you are learning, as you share each day in our group. I particularly like this method of study because it gives me a chance to go back and reread the verses, ponder the observations, review my applications and pray my prayers. I think of it like my journal.

We will be reading one chapter of the Bible each day. We will not be giving you a specific scripture to focus on in that chapter. Your SOAK could look something like this on our thread:

S—Scripture - Verses 1-5 is what stood out to me today (Or—you can actually type out verses 1-5).

O—Observation - Share your basic observations here.

A—Application—How are you going to take what you have learned and apply it?

K—Kneel in Prayer - You don't have to type out your prayer but you can.

I typically share in a paragraph form. Usually my first 2 -3 sentences is an observation and then 2-3 sentences for application.

Basically, there is no right or wrong way to do it. Just share what God has taught you each day!

My SOAK will be posted at the top of the Facebook Group each day. If you miss a day, go back through the threads and catch up if you need to.

PRAYER PHOTO:

On Sunday, I will ask for prayer requests. Please add your prayer requests by commenting. Let us know any answers or updates. Feel free to post prayers for others as well. I will copy your prayer request down in my prayer journal and pray for you often. Please feel free to do the same!

GROUP GUIDELINES

1. This is a commitment. Try to check in daily. Accountability is key.

2. This is a confidential group. What we share here stays here.

3. Please be aware of each others feelings. Be as loving in your comments as you can.

4. When sharing about other family members or friends, be as positive as you can (ie: family issues, marriage problems).

5. PRAY for each other!

6. Grow this session. We want to be stronger when we finish.

PARTICIPATION

Since this is an online community, participation is KEY! To participate means that you do your study and then **share**! If you don't feel comfortable sharing all of the time, you can "like" comments or write encouraging remarks like "that's a great insight." The point is, we want to know you are here, your **participation shows your presence**. I know some of you will be busy, but if you are not involved, then consider taking some time off from the group. The reason for this small group is for everyone to feel they have a voice and each of you are very special. So please participate. If I don't see you participating, I will message you to make sure you are still with us.

ACCOUNTABILITY

Your participation and interaction with the group is vital! Not only will it help you get more out of the study, but your words may be just what someone else needs to hear. We are all accountable to each other, so check in as often as you can.

RESOURCES

- Print off the reading plan and put it into your Bible.

- Get a notebook ready for Bible study. Loose-leaf paper or a journal is fine or, be sure to order your journal from Amazon.

- Remember, the journals on Amazon are journals and not Bible Studies. They do have the discussion questions and a book synopsis for you.

- Watch the blog: ***www.WomenLivingWell.org*** for posts about Good Morning Girls. Courtney will post content on Mondays and Fridays.

- Subscribing to the blog will make sure that you get all the updates!

ENCOURAGEMENT

If you have any questions, please message me. I really want this not only to be a Bible study, but an interactive online caring community as well. This will be a great way to keep connected. I'm so glad you are here in our group!

Much Love,

_____

9 Ways to Get More Out of Your Study

As Christians, one of the most important things that we can do is to study the Word of God.

God's Word is to be a light to our path (Psalm 119:105). It teaches us about God's heart and allows us to know the mind of Christ (Psalm 119:105, Psalm 119, Philippians 2:5). Through the study of God's Word, we can learn how to apply God's Word to our lives, allowing it to be the map we use to guide our lives, and allowing Christ to be the true cornerstone of our life (Ephesians 2:20 KJV).

Here are a few tips on how to study the Bible:

1. Get a Bible that you can write in.

I am not talking about an expensive wide margin with extra pages (although I have one and I love it!), but just a Bible that you feel comfortable writing in or highlighting. I would also suggest getting a box of colored pencils, two notebooks or some loose-leaf paper (and maybe some dividers if you like to be super organized!)

2. Pray. Just like in any other thing that you do in life, you should start your Bible Study with prayer.

The most common thing that I hear is "I just don't understand the Bible."

You should start each study session with prayer. Some of my personal favorites to pray are Psalm 119:18: "Open my eyes, that I may behold wondrous things out of your law." and Psalm 119:130: "The unfolding of your words gives light; it imparts understanding to the simple."

2 Timothy 3:16 tells us, that all Scripture is given by God and is profitable for doctrine, reproof, correction and instruction in righteousness. When I pray, I ask God to show me these things in the passage that I am about to read.

3. Read the passage. Read it again.

You will gain insight through reading it several times. I like to read it quietly, then out loud, and then quietly again.

4. Write the Scripture.

I love how here at GMG we write scripture out. In your SOAK notes, you will only write out a small portion of our text, but I did want to share that writing out Scripture is KEY to studying and learning. I like to skip lines when I write, so I have room to write or draw around the key words, people, places, and themes. It also gives me room to write definitions for words or names. (This is where my colored pencils or highlighters come in.)

5. Pull the passage apart, looking for any names, repeated words, phrases, ideas, and places. (Each one gets its own color.)

Look up the meaning of a name or word in a Concordance. Look for the first time a word is mentioned in Scripture, to get a better understanding of its meaning. Write the meaning and other notes beside the word.

6. Answer key questions when studying the Bible:

Who is the passage written to? For example: the Jews, disciples, the Church/Christians, or non-Christians.

Who wrote it?

When was it written? Was it written in the Old Testament, New Testament or before or after Christ's ascension into Heaven?

Where was it written? Discover if there were any customs or laws that would be common during this time period in this location.

Why was it written? Was it written for doctrine, reproof, correction, or instruction?

How does this passage apply to my life as a follower of Christ? How does my life need to change because of this passage?

Some other great application questions might be: What stood out to me in today's verses? What challenged me? What did I learn? What is God teaching me?

We also provide daily discussion questions for you to use for personal reflection or in your groups.

7. Use resources like Bible commentaries available online for you to read or listen to.

8. Put the Word into practice in your daily life.

Jesus said in Luke 11:28, "But even more blessed are all who hear the Word of God and put it into practice."

9. Have fun!

These questions can help you as you dive into God's Word each day. They go beautifully with the SOAK reading plan. You can use them as you respond in your Observation and Application section.

God's Word is alive.

It is powerful.

It changes lives.

Every time I read a passage, God reveals more to me about WHO He is.

It is a personal love letter written from the lover of my soul and it is the Great Physician's surgical knife, helping me cut out the cancer of sin in my life. It is a light to our path—leading us daily closer to Christ.

Frequently Asked Questions

Q. I was expecting the Journal to be more devotional. Is it necessary to print or buy the journals?

A. No. The Journals available on Amazon are optional and are a place to record your study. It is already broken down into daily readings. You may use your own journal or lined notebook paper if you wish.

Q. What is the difference between the printable journal on the Good Moring Girls Website and the Journal on Amazon.

A. The printable journals are simply divided for you already for your SOAK. You can choose to print them, or use your own paper. The journals on Amazon do not have devotions in them; however, they do have a place for your study, a daily verse, a daily reflection question and a synopsis of the book we are studying. It is your choice to print or buy them—they are not necessary.

Q. Will everyone on my Facebook friends list be able to see my comments in my GMG group, in their news feed, when I post insights or a prayer request?

A. This depends on the group settings. Your posts will only appear in someone else's news feed, if they are currently your friend and a member of the group. We encourage all groups to be set to secret. Facebook settings for this say "Non-members can't find these groups in searches or see anything about the group, including its name and member list. The name of the group will not display on the timelines of members. To join a secret group, you need to be added by a member of the group." Please use discretion about sharing extremely personal details, since anything posted on Facebook still belongs to Facebook.

Q. What is the difference between our SOAK passage and the Verse of the Day?

A. Our SOAK passage is the large passage of scripture, which we are reading for the day. Our Verse of the Day gives us a specific verse to meditate on, should we need help finding something more specific. You can share about any verse in the passage but this verse is helpful for those who are new to Bible study and need a starting point.

Q. What if I do my Bible study but I don't feel like I should share anything that day?

A. Maybe your reflections for the day are super personal. Sharing would be hard because it might expose something that is personal to your family or another person's situation. If you don't feel like you can share insights, make sure you "like" the daily post to let others know you have read that day. (If you are on email, just share that you read). Read the other comments and add encouraging remarks or "likes". It is okay if the same thought is shared several times by several people.

Q. Life got crazy for me. Now I feel discouraged because I am behind and I find it intimidating to catch up. Should I leave the group?

A. NO! Everyone here is growing in their walk with God. None of us our perfect. We all need Him. Start fresh tomorrow and pick up where the group is. Use the weekends or time off on breaks, between sessions, to catch up.

Q. Can I invite friends?

A. YES! We have found that groups run more effectively when people invite their friends, someone they know that they connect with outside of the Internet. Making new friends is great but it is nice to have someone you "know" to process life with.

Icebreaker Questions

These are optional, and just a fun way to get to know your group. You can use these questions weekly or just at the beginning of a session.

Post a picture of your family and tell us about them.

Post a favorite recipe (break it up breakfast, lunch, dinner, snack, dessert).

Post a quote you love.

Share your favorite verse.

Share your favorite Bible character.

Where in the world have you lived?

Where would you like to live?

What languages do you speak or do you want to speak?

What makes you laugh?

What are you afraid of?

What is your favorite book?

What is your favorite season?

What is your favorite childhood memory?

What is your favorite room in your house?

What is your favorite place to vacation?

What is your favorite vacation memory?

Is Your Good Morning Girls Group Struggling?
~A FINAL NOTE OF ENCOURAGEMENT FROM COURTNEY

We have heard that some groups are doing amazing and dynamic! Praise the Lord! But we have also heard that some groups are struggling. So I thought I would write to encourage those who may be struggling.

Here are a few issues you could be facing:

1. You feel like you are emailing or Facebooking yourself every morning.

If the rest of your group is not responding daily, do not be discouraged. Though you are missing out on the vibrant and deep spiritual conversation you were looking forward to, God has put this group together for a reason. Continue to rise early and commune with God. You are being blessed by this time. I believe that those who receive your emails and Facebook messages are getting a tidbit of God's truth spoken into their lives, through you. So persevere. When the end of this session comes, pray about trying again with a new group.

2. Two or three in your group email or Facebook consistently and the others are not participating. You wonder if you should confront those ladies.

I would not confront them but I would let them know that they are missed and that you would love to hear from them more, to connect. Some ladies are going to struggle more than others based on their season of life, their ability to be disciplined and their willingness to open up in a small group. Pray for the ladies and be patient with them.

3. You feel like some in the group are judgmental or just different from you. You aren't connecting.

Sometimes this is "iron sharpening iron"(Proverbs 27:17). It can hurt at times to be stretched and grow. But sometimes this is someone else's problem and has nothing to do with you. Their personality and disposition is just difficult. All of us are on a journey toward growth and some need more grace than others. Be a giver of grace in the group. Cover this girl in prayer.

4. You want out!

The guilt of failing to have your own quiet time is frustrating.

Don't give up. Give yourself grace! God loves you deeply and no matter what you do good or bad, He will always love you. Do not heap guilt on yourself but take baby steps towards growth. If all you can do is read one verse a day, then do it! Start there and move forward. Pray and ask God for a hunger, thirst and discipline to be in his Word.

5. You love the concept but want a new group.

A new session is always right around the corner. Hang tight and when this session ends, join us again and try a new group. Really pray about whom God would bring into your next group and open it up to new ladies from on-line. Simply leave a comment out on the blog, that you have an open group, and ladies from around the globe will join you.

6. Your group is too large and the messages are too much.

Look for a second leader inside your group. When the next session begins, divide your group into two groups. It may be hard to do this but it will benefit everyone to be able to manage all the messages and respond and connect. Pray that your group will be willing to do this.

Please know your struggles in your group are normal. My own group has gone through many changes over the years. As seasons changed, women left, new ones joined and old ones returned. Keep leaning on Jesus for wisdom and strength. He is with you and will guide you!

Thank you for leading! We serve a worthy Savior!

Walk with the King,

Courtney

This manual is dedicated to Mandy Kelly.

Mandy was the GMG Leadership Coordinator for many years.

She was a friend and encourager to all the women in the GMG Ministry.

We are so grateful for her ministry here and she is greatly missed.

Mandy is with Jesus now and I can't wait to be reunited with her in heaven.

But we do not want you to be uninformed, brothers, about those who are asleep,
that you may not grieve as others do who have no hope.
For since we believe that Jesus died and rose again, even so, through Jesus,
God will bring with him those who have fallen asleep.
1 Thessalonians 4:13,14

Made in the USA
San Bernardino, CA
02 January 2018